W9-AAG-990

Mountains and Volcanoes

Written by Eileen Curran

Illustrated by James Watling

Troll Associates

Library of Congress Cataloging in Publication Data

Curran, Eileen.
    Mountains and volcanoes.

    Summary: Explains in simple language how mountains
change and form, and how some begin as volcanoes.
    1. Mountains—Juvenile literature.   2. Volcanoes—
Juvenile literature.   [1. Mountains.   2. Volcanoes]
I. Watling, James, ill.   II. Title.
GB512.C87   1985   551.4'32   84-8638
ISBN 0-8167-0347-7 (lib. bdg.)
ISBN 0-8167-0348-5 (pbk.)

Copyright © 1985 by Troll Associates, Mahwah, New Jersey
All rights reserved. No part of this book may be used
or reproduced in any manner whatsoever without written
permission from the publisher.
Printed in the United States of America

10 9 8 7 6 5 4 3 2 1

High, high up!

What do you see?

It is a mountain.

How wonderful it can be.

High, high up.

Mountains are always changing.

Year after year, the wind and the rain

slowly wear mountains away.

But new mountains are forming.
(Some of the biggest are under the sea.)

Can you guess how mountains form?

From deep down inside,
the earth pulls and pushes.

It tugs,
and squeezes,
and slowly folds
the land.

The earth pushes and pulls up.

The earth pushes and falls down.

And as it moves...

a new mountain can slowly form.

What's happening now?
Some mountains begin with a boom!

Some mountains begin as a volcano.

Just look inside the earth!
Hot melted rock, called lava, is building up.

Then it pushes and shoots out the top!

When the lava cools and hardens...

it will become part of the new mountain.

Mountains are always changing.

They change every day.

But new mountains are forming.

They are forming today.

High, high up — as far as you can see.

It is a mountain.

How wonderful it can be!